This Cursive Handwriting Workbook engaging sections.

In this section, your child may trace large dotted letters first. They can then trace the smaller letters and practice writing the letters in the lines.

In this section, your child will learn to write words in cursive. They can start with simple two- and three-letter words. They can then move on to more complex four-, five-, six-letter words, and so on.

In this section, your child will learn to write full sentences in cursive. Who says it has to be so boring? These sentences are some funny jokes, riddles, and language puzzles!

How to write cursive *a* (small):

a a a a a a a a a a

How to write cursive *a* (capital):

a a a a a a a a a

a a a a a a a a

a a a a a a a a

a a a

a

a a a a a a a

a a a

a

ABCDEFGHIJKLMNOPQRSTUVWXYZ

Practice Page

How to write cursive *b* (small):

b b b b b b b b b b

How to write cursive *B* (capital):

B B B B B B B B B

b b b b b b b b

b b b b b b b b

b b b

b

B B B B B B B

B B B

B

Practice Page

How to write cursive c (small):

c c c c c c c c c c c c c

How to write cursive C (capital):

C C C C C C C C C

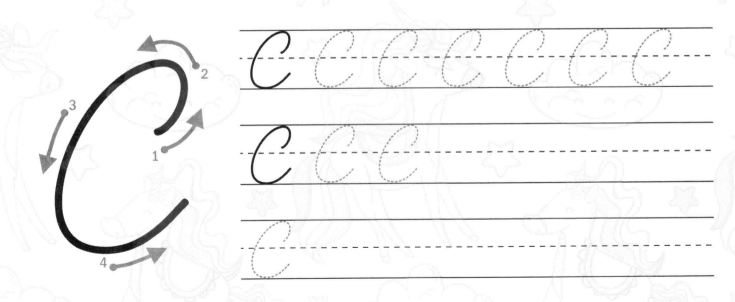

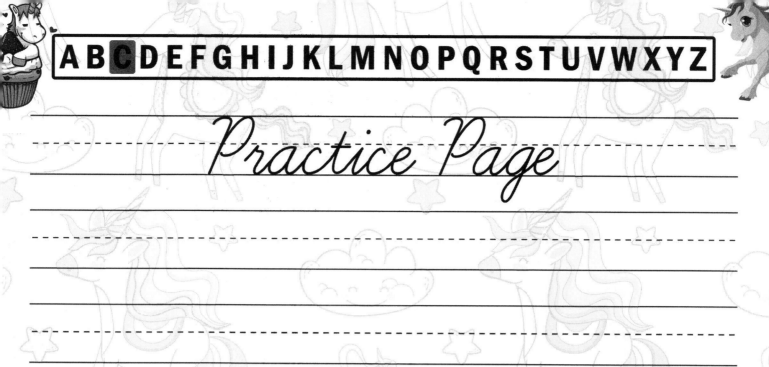

ABCDEFGHIJKLMNOPQRSTUVWXYZ

Practice Page

How to write cursive *d* (small):

d d d d d d d d d d

How to write cursive *D* (capital):

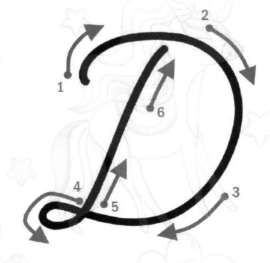

D D D D D D D D D D

Practice Page

How to write cursive *e* (small):

e e e e e e e e e e

How to write cursive *E* (capital):

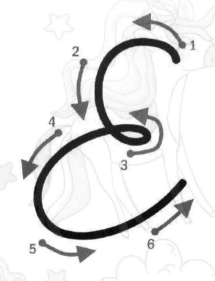

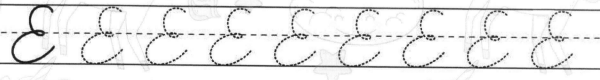

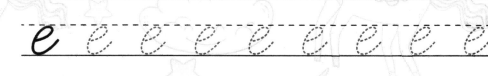

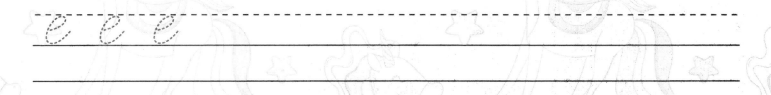

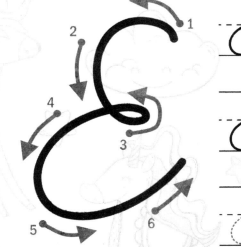

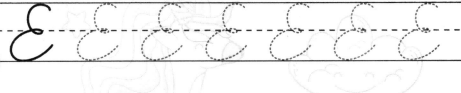

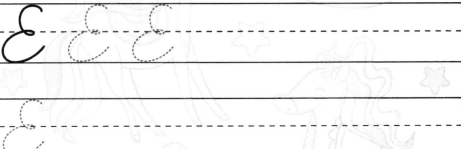

A B C D E F G H I J K L M N O P Q R S T U V W X Y Z

Practice Page

How to write cursive *f* (small):

f f f f f f f f f f f f

How to write cursive *F* (capital):

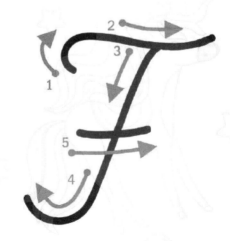

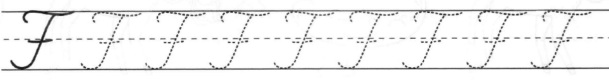

A B C D E F G H I J K L M N O P Q R S T U V W X Y Z

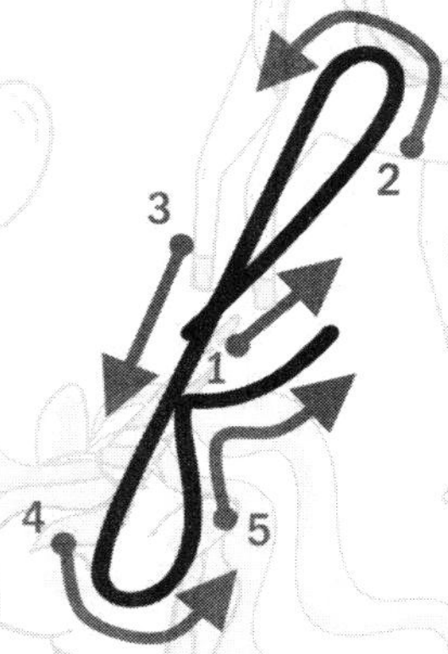

f f f f f f f f f

f f f f f f f f f

f f f

f

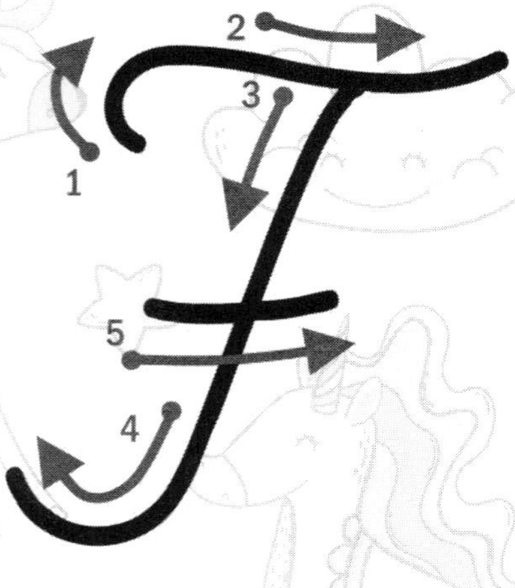

F F F F F F F

F F F

F

Practice Page

How to write cursive *g* (small):

g g g g g g g g g g

How to write cursive *G* (capital):

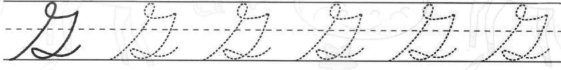

Practice Page

How to write cursive *h* (small):

h h h h h h h h h

How to write cursive *H* (capital):

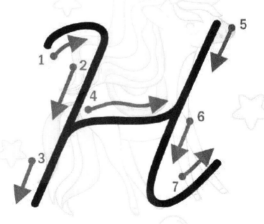

H H H H H H H H

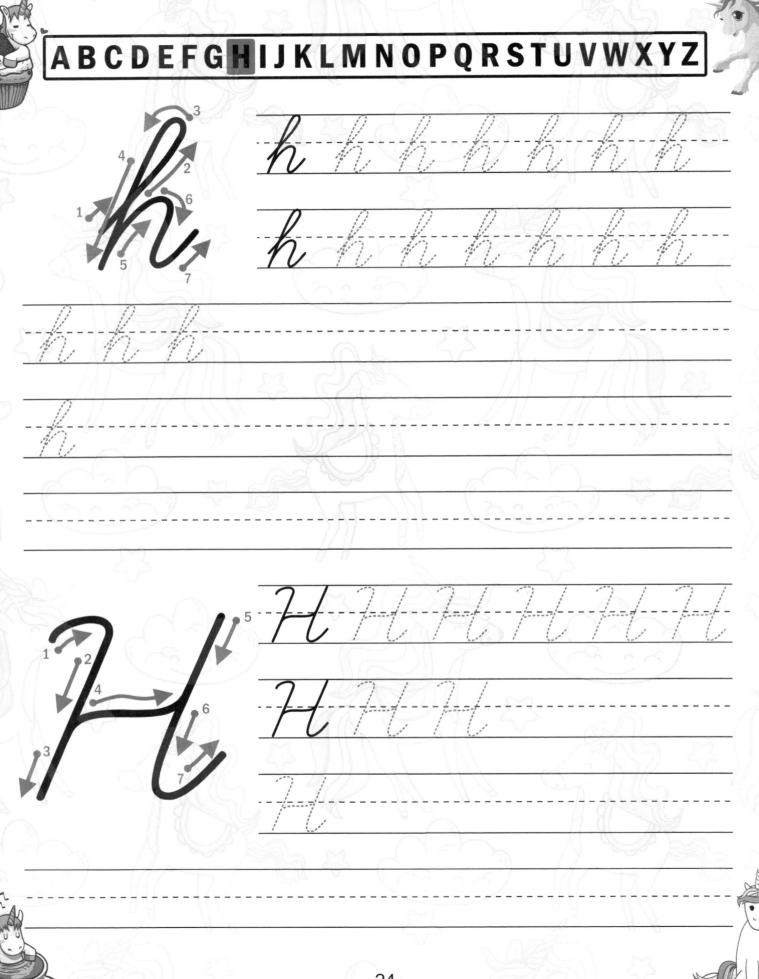

Practice Page

How to write cursive *i* (small):

i i i i i i i i i i i i i i i

How to write cursive *l* (capital):

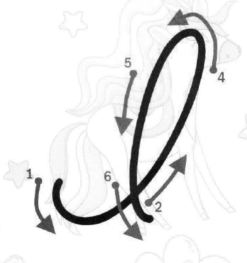

l l l l l l l l l l l

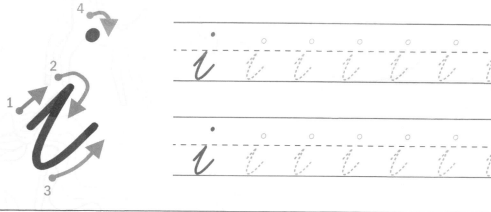

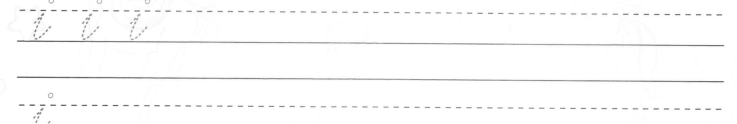

Practice Page

How to write cursive *j* (small):

How to write cursive *J* (capital):

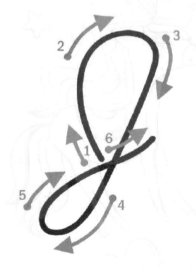

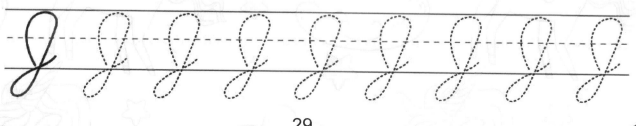

ABCDEFGHIJKLMNOPQRSTUVWXYZ

Practice Page

How to write cursive k (small):

How to write cursive K (capital):

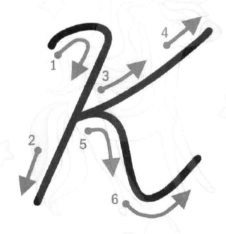

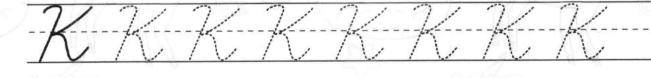

k k k k k k k k

k k k k k k k k

k k k

k

K K K K K K

K K K

K

A B C D E F G H I J **K** L M N O P Q R S T U V W X Y Z

Practice Page

How to write cursive *l* (small):

How to write cursive *L* (capital):

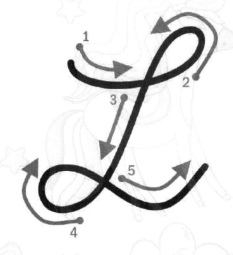

Practice Page

How to write cursive *m* (small):

m m m m m m m

How to write cursive *M* (capital):

M M M M M M M

Practice Page

How to write cursive n (small):

n n n n n n n n

How to write cursive N (capital):

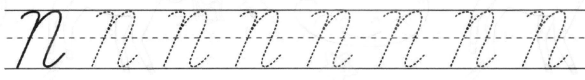

Practice Page

How to write cursive *o* (small):

How to write cursive *O* (capital):

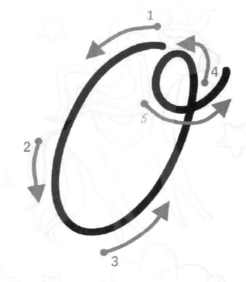

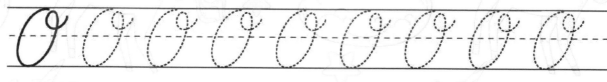

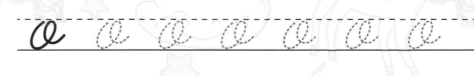

ABCDEFGHIJKLMN**O**PQRSTUVWXYZ

Practice Page

How to write cursive p (small):

How to write cursive P (capital):

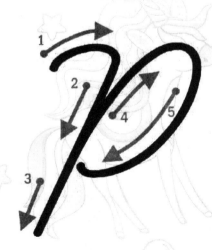

p p p p p p p p

p p p p p p p p

p p p

p

P P P P P P P P

P P P

P

ABCDEFGHIJKLMNO**P**QRSTUVWXYZ

Practice Page

How to write cursive *q* (small):

q q q q q q q q q q q

How to write cursive *Q* (capital):

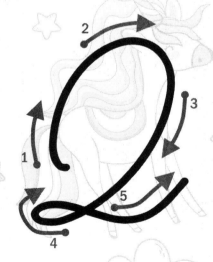

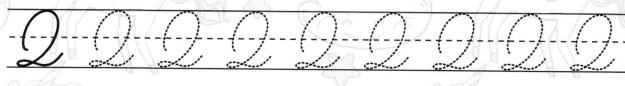

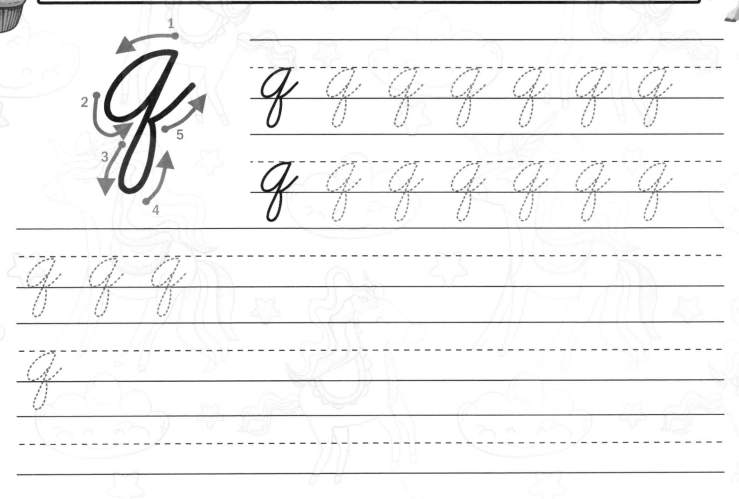

Practice Page

How to write cursive 𝓇 (small):

𝓇 𝓇 𝓇 𝓇 𝓇 𝓇 𝓇 𝓇 𝓇

How to write cursive 𝓡 (capital):

𝓡 𝓡 𝓡 𝓡 𝓡 𝓡 𝓡 𝓡

ABCDEFGHIJKLMNOPQRSTUVWXYZ

Practice Page

How to write cursive *s* (small):

How to write cursive *S* (capital):

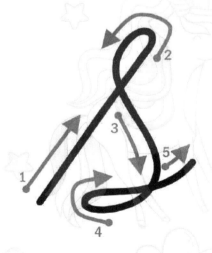

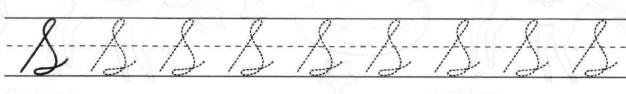

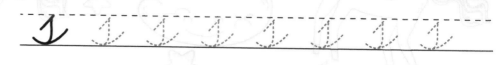

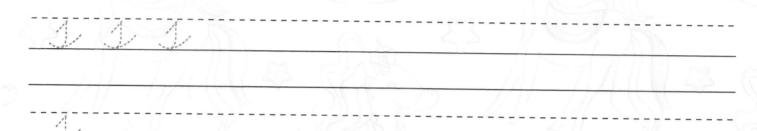

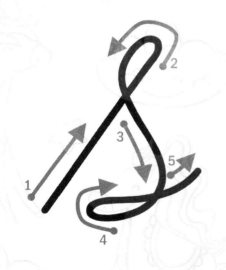

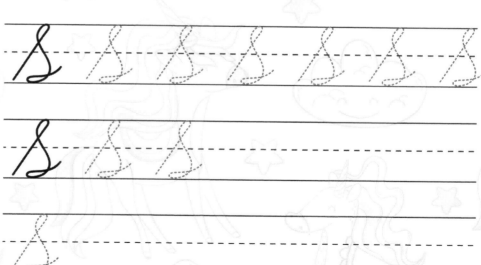

ABCDEFGHIJKLMNOPQR**S**TUVWXYZ

Practice Page

How to write cursive *t* (small):

t t t t t t t t t t t

How to write cursive *T* (capital):

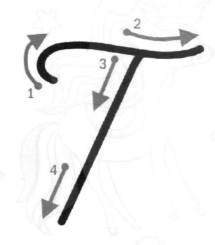

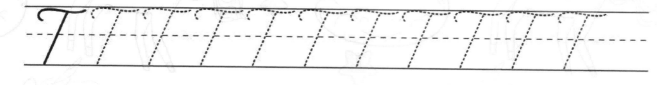

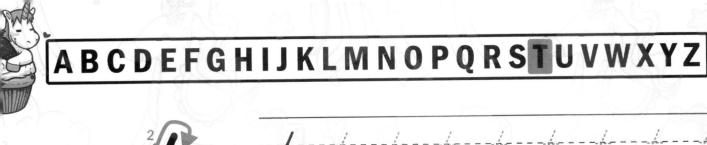

t t t t t t t t t t

t t t t t t t t t t

t t t

t

T T T T T T T

T T T

T

Practice Page

How to write cursive u (small):

u u u u u u u u u u

How to write cursive $\mathcal{U}$ (capital):

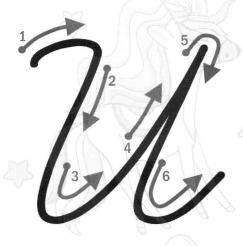

$\mathcal{U}$ $\mathcal{U}$ $\mathcal{U}$ $\mathcal{U}$ $\mathcal{U}$ $\mathcal{U}$ $\mathcal{U}$

u u u u u u u

u u u u u u u

u u u

u

U U U U U U

U U U

U

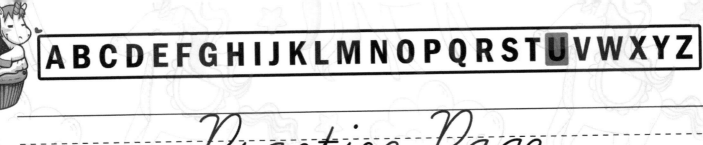

Practice Page

How to write cursive *u* (small):

How to write cursive *V* (capital):

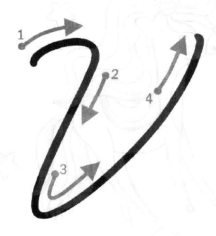

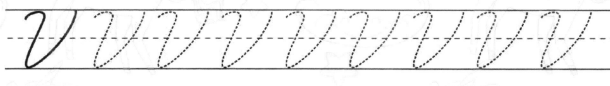

Practice Page

How to write cursive  (small):

How to write cursive 𝒲 (capital):

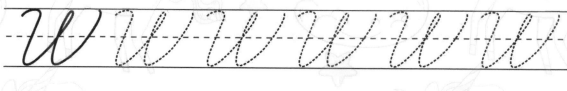

A B C D E F G H I J K L M N O P Q R S T U V W X Y Z

Practice Page

How to write cursive x (small):

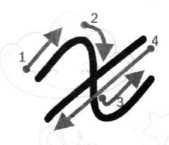

x x x x x x x x x x x

How to write cursive X (capital):

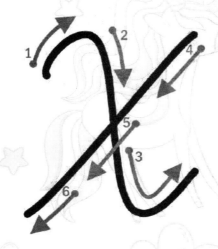

X X X X X X X X X X X

Practice Page

How to write cursive *y* (small):

y y y y y y y y y

How to write cursive *Y* (capital):

Y Y Y Y Y Y Y Y Y

ABCDEFGHIJKLMNOPQRSTUVWXYZ

Practice Page

How to write cursive *z* (small):

How to write cursive *Z* (capital):

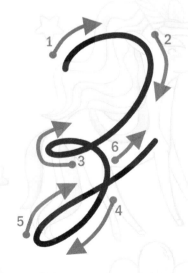

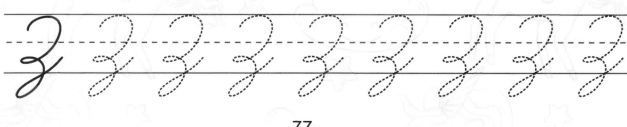

Practice Page

a c ac ac

b e be be

c a ca ca

d o do do

e a ea ea

f i fi fi

g e ge ge

h e he he

i f if if

How to connect cursive letters

j a ja ja

k l kl kl

l d ld ld

m g mg mg

n h h nh nh

o k ok ok

p n pn pn

q u qu qu

r s rs rs

s i si si

t u tu tu

u l ul ul

u m um um

u r ur ur

x c xc xc

y k yk yk

z y zy zy

are are

cat cat

dad dad

get get

how how

may may

not not

one one

put put

she she

How to connect uppercase letters in cursive

And

But

Can

Day

Has

Mrs

Now

Our

Red

How to connect uppercase letters in cursive

See

Two

Use

Was

You

Eat

For

Let

Who

all all

big big

come come

did did

from from

him him

is is

in in

it it

look look

mum mum

out out

play play

run run

Writing words in cursive

said said

the the

up up

Writing words in cursive

want want

yes yes

after after

back back

could could

down down

every every

find find

good good

have have

little little

make make

people people

round round

some some

under under

Writing words in cursive

yellow yellow

children children

please please

number number

I can write words in

cursive now. It is fun!

I will write sentences in

cursive now. Let's do it.

What goes up when

rain comes down?

An umbrella

When do monkeys fall

from the sky?

During APril showers

What month of the year

is the shortest?

May (only three letters)

What's full of holes but

still holds water?

A sponge

What belongs to you but

is used more by others?

Your name

I am full of keys, but

can't open any door.

What am I?

A piano

What has hands but

can't clap?

A clock

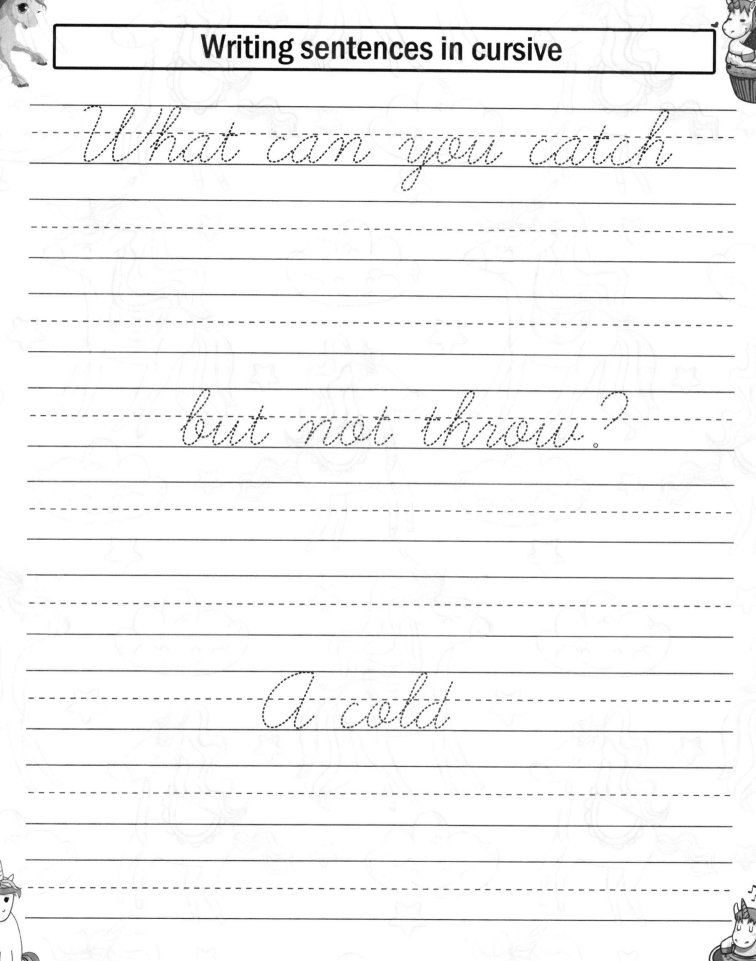

What can you catch

but not throw?

A cold

What has 4 eyes but

can't see?

Mississippi

What is at the center

of gravity?

The letter V

What two things can you

never eat for breakfast?

Lunch and dinner

How do oceans say

hello to each other?

They wave!

Writing sentences in cursive

What keys can't open

any door?

A monkey and a donkey

What music frightens

balloons? Pop music

I scream, you scream,

we all scream,

for ice cream!

I saw a kitten eating

chicken in the kitchen.

Why is B so cool?

Because it is sitting in AC

What letter is always wet?

C!

What starts with T, ends

with T and is filled with T?

Teapot